How to Bribe a Judge

Poems from the Bench

How to Bribe a Judge

Poems from the Bench

JAMES CLARKE

TORONTO

Exile Editions
2002

This edition is published by Exile Editions Limited,
20 Dale Avenue, Toronto, Ontario, Canada M4W 1K4

Sales Distribution:
McArthur & Company
c/o Harper Collins
1995 Markham Road
Toronto, ON
M1B 5M8
toll free:
1 800 387 0117
(fax) 1 800 668 5788

Composition & Design by *Michael Callaghan*
Cover Concept by *Tim Hanna*
Typeset at *Moons of Jupiter Inc.*
Cover Photograph by *Julia McArthur*
Author Photograph by *John Reeves*
Printed and Bound by *Transcontinental Printing*

ONTARIO ARTS COUNCIL
CONSEIL DES ARTS DE L'ONTARIO

The Canada Council for the Arts since 1957 | Le Conseil des Arts du Canada depuis 1957

The publisher wishes to acknowledge the assistance toward publication of the Canada Council and the Ontario Arts Council.

ISBN 1-55096-558-1

To my colleagues
on the Bench

Rule of Law

Status, power, money
like straw, feathers, dust
are insubstantial things,

but if they all blow one way
that's the way the law bends.

(after W. Stafford)

Contents

INTRODUCTION

For a long time in Canada, law and literature have been closely associated. Many lawyers like Morley Torgov, Guy Gavriel Kay and William Deverall are novelists. Some lawyers like F.R. Scott, A.M. Klein and Edward Douglas Armour have been poets. So it is not surprising to discover that there is a person in Canada, both poet and judge. As you will see from this collection of poetry, James Clarke is a genuine poetic Justice! His judicial activities and thoughts find expression in his poetry. His free verse is direct, understandable, honest, entertaining and rich with insight into the law and the human condition. He proves the old saying, "Even as there are laws of poetry, so there is poetry in law." If poetry is writing that is destined to live beyond the immediate hour, then the Honourable Justice James Clarke of the Ontario Superior Court of Justice has written true poetry and has made a lasting contribution to the law and to literature.

For many, it will be comforting to learn from this collection of poems that judges are people who remain very human even after assuming their judicial duties. Like the rest of humankind, judges may be affected from time to time by pride and passion, by pettiness and bruised feelings, by misunderstanding and by excessive zeal. But what we learn, above all else, is that judges are not always dull and solemn even though their courtrooms are often filled with the world of the grim and sorrowful. The stark reality of the legal system is packed with perplexities and absurdities. Judges are beset by weighty decisions that have to be made and important issues that have to be resolved, and it is interesting to get some insight into the judicial mind. Judges must be possessed of many virtues: integrity, patience, courtesy, kindness, compassion, wisdom and an even temper. Justice Clarke cares about justice. This judge is humorous, witty, tender, sympathetic and has an attractive humility. When he was a schoolboy, he was falsely accused by a classmate of stealing seventy-five cents ("Falsely Accused"). To his credit, he has never forgotten the pain of that experience and wonders if the accused person before him is also suffering that pain.

Judge Clarke may care about the accused persons, but he also cares about the victims. He sees all the miseries and he feels sorry for everybody. As a judge, all humanity with all its warts appears before him. He is very upset that people molest children. Yet, he has pity for the "not-so-good thief" and believes "there has to be a place / in paradise even for the clumsy thief / whose simplicity / makes us want to forgive / like Jesus, / his artless mischief." ("Sometimes I Feel Pity.")

Justice Clarke's poems are a pleasure to read. They are well-written, thoughtful and contemplative. His poems give an insight into the thoughts of a judge, insight that one wouldn't be able to get elsewhere. One gets a real sense of both the best and the worst of judging. In his poems, the best of judging is reflected in his pursuit of justice and the power to set things right. The worst of judging is reflected at times when, even though the system is impossible to fix and decisions are impossible to make, the law still commands the judge to take a side, whether he wants to or not.

Some of his poems are stories of the colourful people who have appeared before him ("Addiction," "Believe Me Judge, There Are Days When I Can Hardly Believe Myself," and "A Question Too Far") or marvels of how the world is changing ("Strange Encounters of a New Kind"). Some are about the difficult job of sentencing ("A Certain Image") and some about the experience of being in court ("Nervousness in Court").

There are poems where the judge speaks of humbling moments, such as when he asks a lawyer to rise in the courtroom, not knowing that he is disabled ("An Embarrassing Moment"), and when the judge threatens to punch another lawyer in the nose ("An Egregious Indiscretion"). This poet reveals himself in these poems as so human, making mistakes like all the rest of us. You want to be in his company.

No one has written in a more compelling fashion about the independence of the judiciary than Clarke in "A Judge's Progress." When he was appointed a judge, he wrote "judgments / To follow the Law / And please the Court of Appeal." When the appellate court overruled him, "he knew he was doing something wrong." But, as he grew in his job, "he wrote judgments / to please himself / and follow the Court of Conscience. / Now when the Court of Appeal disagreed, / he knew / he was doing something right."

Francis Bacon, when he was Lord Chancellor of England, was removed from office for accepting a litigant's bribe. Despite its provocative title, Clarke's book will not help the future Bacons of this world to avoid getting caught for their grave misconduct. "How to Bribe a Judge" describes bribery by flattery, by laughing "heartily at all his jokes even when / they're incomprehensible," by finishing "every / sentence with My Lord" or "You're one step ahead of me / as usual My Lord," by telling the judge "his judgments are novel, break / new ground" and by never appealing his judgments.

In this poem the true James Clarke is revealed. He sees everything. Only the innocent would want him as their judge. If lawyers follow "How to Bribe a Judge", they should never forget what Harold R. Medina once said in "Some Reflections on the Judicial Function: A Personal Viewpoint," 38 *ABAJ* (1952), 107, 108: "After all is said and done, we cannot deny the fact that a judge is almost of necessity surrounded by people who keep telling him what a wonderful fellow he is. And if he once begins to believe it, he is a lost soul." Clarke is no lost soul.

Edward L. Greenspan, Q.C.
Toronto, Ontario
May, 2002

How to Bribe

Poems from the Bench

a Judge

Poetry

It started innocently enough,
a few rhyming couplets,

but soon the judge began to devour words,
found he could no longer sleep
and would wake up, words dripping from his mouth.

He grew thinner
but didn't care
for he was supremely happy, like
fishing in a deep, mysterious lake,

but then, too late, he noticed some words
were stones and his
papers became blotted with blood.
His daughter phoned the doctor.

At first the hospital wasn't so bad until
he started to steal pens and write
sonnets on meal forms and
clean white bedsheets; worse, he began to
wake up at night shouting for a rhyming
dictionary, disturbing other
patients, creating a backlash
against poetry.

That's when the doctors
decided to move him to another ward
where he was strapped into a steel bed.
Diagnosis: TEMPORARY INSANITY.
DICTIONARIES FORBIDDEN.

The Race to Paradise

Before God created
                man
She took
                a chunk of coal
from the coalbin
and scratched
                a thin line
across the void,
                counted off
seven days
                and seven nights,
and hurled a star
                against
the sky
                (O what a bang!)
                to announce
the start of
                the race to paradise.
That's when men
                began to murder one another.

Addiction

His biceps are covered with tattoos:
                                        daggers, swastikas, the Grim
Reaper.
He used to sell drugs.
He was hooked on crystal methamphetamines.

The serial killer sits in a cell
                                        surrounded by multi-
coloured
skeins of yarn. All day
he knits beanie caps, teddy bears, dolls, scarves &
                                        mittens for homeless children.
He's been knitting for nine years.

Touch his needles & he'll break your teeth.

Blackout

I enter the windowless courtroom,
take my seat behind the bench
with full knowledge the circuitry
is faulty. Still I'm disturbed
when the lights go out—the sixth
time this month—plunging police,
witnesses, reporters, public, every-
one into blackness. My deputy,
who is used to such happenings, gives
me a flashlight—one of those long
Maglites. What to do? I know it will
take months, maybe years to fix the
system. The Crown insists that the case
proceed: Justice delayed, Justice
denied, she argues.

And so testimony is taken;
my Maglite criss-crosses
the darkness, catching startled eyes,
the guilty everywhere—nowhere.

Gulls

A flock of gulls settled
in the brown field next
to the courthouse this morning,

squealed and pecked
in the wet grass
then veered away
against a pewter sky.

A Bump the Size of a Dime

Until his accident, the plaintiff
led a normal life. The damage was so minor—
dent in the trunk—police were not called. The
doctor who examined his injuries—a bump on the forehead
the size of a dime—prescribed Tylenol III, told him to get some rest.

But he got migraines, couldn't eat, couldn't
sleep. X-rays, CAT-scans, MRIs proved
negative. He quit driving, stopped bowling,
missed work. He found he could no longer make
love to his wife. The psychiatrist diagnosed
anxiety; he tried acupuncture, massages,
home exercises but nothing worked. Eventually
lost his job, spent most days holed up in the basement
watching game shows. When his wife couldn't take it any longer,
she packed her bags, grabbed the kids,
and moved out.

Last week his lawyer came to court seeking a million dollars.
"My client was born with a thin skull," he said.

A Certain Image

haunts the judge's dreams.
Standing over a deep well
he grips the ankles of the guilty
and before he lets go
glimpses terror
on their faces.
Then, pity ticking in his ear,
he leans his head
into the rounded darkness,
listening
for the splash.

A Young Offender

He was only eighteen,
with the baby face of a teenager,
when he appeared
charged with twelve counts
of armed robbery.

During the bail hearing he stared through me
as though
I were glass.

Not once did his eyes
betray the blue fury
inside him, even when
I refused bail.

Yes, he would go away for awhile
but I knew he'd be back,
older and deadlier
and I was scared,
the same dread the crew
of the *Enola Gay* felt
as they dropped their dark and
awkward child on the dreaming city.

Falsely Accused

When the judge was a schoolboy a classmate
falsely accused him of stealing seventy-
five cents. The more
he protested his innocence the more
he was disbelieved,
caged in guilt, a victim
of unfairness.

Now when an accused takes the stand
he looks for clues: inflection,
tone of voice, a particular expression,
any reminder of what it was like
to be charged with something
you didn't do.

An Embarrassing Moment

He believed in the
ceremony and trappings
of judicial protocol:
the ring of "Oyez, Oyez"
to open Court, the deferential
nicety of "Your Honour,"
the silk robes,
the authority of the
red sash.

That's why he was disturbed
when one lawyer at the counsel
table failed to rise.

"It's customary in our courts to
stand when a judge enters the
court," he said glowering.

But when he observed the lawyer
lean sideways, pick up the cane
beside his chair
and painfully
struggle to rise, he wished
he could have hidden himself
in the holding cells below.

After the Rape

the doctor's mothering hands
searched her body carefully for signs,
but all he could find was a
discolouration—a "purple
flower" he called it—on her left thigh.
"Superficial," he said
trying to reassure her. "In three weeks
you'll never know it was there."

What the doctor could not see
was the bruise
deep inside,
a blood dark cell
that would multiply and multiply
into starless nights.

Justice Delayed

He was almost eighty,
shaky and forgetful,
when the law
hauled him to court, wheelchair and all.

He couldn't associate the woman
in the witness box with the teenager who
once worked for him nor fathom
her complaint: wordless fondlings
in the dark behind
a storeroom door & he was at a loss
to explain
the long fever of her pain, or
why she'd only complained now that he
was old and sick.

He concluded life was playing him
one last trick.

A Judge's Progress

At the beginning he wrote judgments
to follow the Law
and please the Court of Appeal.

Then when the Court of Appeal disagreed
he knew
he was doing something wrong.

At the end he wrote judgments
to please himself
and follow the Court of Conscience.

Now when the Court of Appeal disagreed,
he knew
he was doing something right.

Diptych

The old orthopaedic expert
called by the defence in the whiplash case
explained the coloured illustrations
of bone, nerve, ligament, tendon, and muscle
of the cervical spine.
"Experiments with monkeys demonstrate," he testified,
"that neck muscles are stronger than steel."

Memories haunted the old judge:
the haste of the hangman's small hands,
a muffled cry,
the echo in a hollow stairwell
after the trap was tripped
and a stillness that settled
over the prison like snow.

Yellow Roses

He couldn't remember
the party,
the boss's warning
to "take it easy,"
stopping at the curb
to buy a dozen yellow roses
from the clown
with a purple nose and red hair,
daydreaming
as he rolled along
about the surprise
he'd planned for their anniversary
—dinner at Angelo's, her favourite
restaurant—
trying to imagine
how pleased she'd be,

nor the red light he failed
to see,
the ball of air
ballooning in his face,
yellow petals scattered
across the asphalt,

nor telling the officer
the light was green,
he'd only had a couple,
it was the other driver's fault,

or the ride back to the station,
white moons
spinning inside his skull,

only
the chafing morning light,
the coldness of the cell,
the officer looming near the bed,
the words
like cold blue steel
crashing through his head.

Lemon Aid

For years the judge had urged litigants
to settle their differences, explained the
folly of seeking perfect justice. One
day it dawned on him that his message
wasn't getting through. He produced
a lemon & a bowl of milk. Holding
the comestible aloft he announced:
"This lemon & the law are first cousins
of the sun, source of light." He cut open &
handed the halves to each party.
"Swallow." The acidity curled their lips.
"A drop of lemon in milk is the cure
for scurvy & optimism," the judge said,
closing his fist on another lemon.

Judging

Sometimes you feel
like an embalmer

with a dull blade
hacking into thick

red meat.
People avert their eyes

from our bloody trade.
Come the revolution

heads will surely roll.

Adjudication

Arrayed in robe and sash
the judge marched past
the razor wire,
knocked on the gate,
announced
he'd come to adjudicate.
"We've been waiting
a long time,"
the director said,
led him on a tour
of kitchen, laundry,
cell and gym,
all the way to
the dark stairwell
in segregation wing;
then as inmates began
to cheer
took out the hood.
"But I'm the law,"
the judge cried.

"That's what they all say."

Prayer for Justice

Bring the clear mirror,
let her see
the jaded eye,
the unforgiving mouth,
let her face break down in tears.

Give back her brown nakedness,
her four, strong limbs,
let her breathe freely,
break softly into new fields.

Act of Mercy

She was convinced the toothpaste had infested the house.
Gobs of it kept appearing on floor, sofa, coffee table,

beds, children's clothing, everywhere, even in the food.
She spent days scrubbing floors, scouring pots and pans,

disinfecting walls; she complained of canker
sores, headaches, abdominal pains. But when she told

her husband, he said she should see a shrink.
The woman from the Health Department, who inspected

the house and found nothing, said it was all in
her head. The manufacturer sent her a list of the

ingredients, all non-toxic, disclaimed responsibility.
Her psychiatrist diagnosed depression, prescribed

Paxil. She persuaded her husband to move, finally
—they looked at dozens of houses—but the virus,

as she called it, always followed her. When the children
began to complain of nightmares, nausea and other pains,

she told neighbours the virus had penetrated
their skin, was eating their intestines and would

eventually pop out their eyes and kill them. She couldn't
sleep, began to see flashing lights. She felt

isolated, misunderstood, trapped in a house of horror.
At her trial, she testified she had no choice.

What mother could allow her children to suffer?

In a Penal Colony

(Port Arthur, Van Diemen's Land)

Francis Curtis, of Exeter, stealing a pair of shoes, seven years.
James Coyne, of Leeds, stealing a canister of tea, seven years.
Thomas Challin, of Kent, stealing two looking glasses, life.
Joseph Crapp, of Devon, stealing a loaf of bread, fourteen years.
John Frederick, of Devon, stealing a Bible, fourteen years.
Richard Dunn, of Cornwall, stealing a bundle of candles, seven years.
Robert Davies, of Sussex, stealing a pocket handkerchief, life.
Charles Chapman, of Essex, stealing a turkey, fourteen years.

William Yoeman, of Shropshire, pickpocketing, seven years.
Felix Daley, of Liverpool, stealing silver spoons, fourteen years.
James Boxhall, of Sussex, pickpocketing a gentleman, life.
William Lacey Cooper, of the Old Bailey, stealing a flute, life.

An Egregious Indiscretion

Whether it was the heat
(the air conditioner had broken down)
or the time (the end of a long,
litigious day)
or simply the bold demeanour of the lawyer
who kept popping up to object
to every ruling,
is difficult to say.

What is clear is that the judge
lost his cool and threatened
to come down from the bench and punch the
lawyer on the nose,
thereby breaching the first judicial
commandment, detachment,

a mistake that the judge
immediately repented
(judges have had to resign for less),
which prompted him
to embark on a course of damage
limitation,

stating for the record
that his words were never meant to be taken
literally,
that he had no intention to hit
the lawyer

and how in any case
his bench was at least 20 feet from the
counsel table, with a huge desk, 3′ x 6′ between,
that even if he'd been serious the feat
would have been impossible.

Then the judge (who had been a boxer
in his youth) added a
final humiliation to his retreat
by pointing out that the lawyer was twice
his size and half his age,
and that such a threat would not only have been
foolhardy,
but patently disastrous.

Which proves that
though a judge's fires may be banked
they're never completely out.

Second Coming

"Don't you know who I am?" said the
accused smiling at the judge incredulously.
"I'm Jesus Christ come back to judge
the world."

For one crazy second the stunned
judge, a firm believer in
the Second Coming, wondered if it might
be true.
Then he said: "Since you obviously know not
what you do, I'm tempted to forgive you,
but I can't. First witness."

Nervousness in Court

I never understood
why witnesses felt fluttery and

fearful in the witness box until
that sunny Friday afternoon

when the OPP cruiser pulled up
alongside me on the Hanlon Expressway

and the officer kept glancing
in my direction

as we rolled along together
well within the speed limit

and I, too, became fluttery
and fearful, wondering

what I'd done wrong (I remember
instinctively checking the seat belt),

amazed in retrospect, after the cruiser
turned off at the next

intersection, how much guilt
we carry and how quickly

innocence can wilt under
the eye of power.

Fog

Driving to Court
this morning,
the fog rose up,
plunging me into a night
streaked with moons
and comets,
all my bright intentions.

His Deputy

When you were ordained Father,
the bishop anointed your hands
with chrism, empowered you to call
down heaven to our earthly table.

In Jesus' name you taught the
Kingdom to little ones—
you were His deputy, a priest
of the Order of Melchisedek,

beloved by all. Then tell me Father
what went wrong? Whose shadow
stalked your light these many years
behind tall rectory walls?

What Eden did you hope to find
within those slender loins,
those sweet red mouths? Today
you appear before me, hands cuffed,

the dark despoiler of God's unlucky
children, and I must lead you
to a place you would not go, a tree
of thorns—broken bread, spilt wine.

The Judge's Fountain Pen

Mute, I lie on the bench,
a eunuch, always
at his beck and call.

When he clasps me between
his fingers, power
bolts down my veins,

my chin trembles. He admires
my ebony shine, the gold
nib, likes to boast

how indispensable I am.
I instill confidence,
make him feel important.

Sometimes he forgets
to fill me, loses his cool
when I can't

perform. How humiliating
to be brushed aside
for a ballpoint!

When he conscripts me
into a bad decision I feel
miserable, itch to stain

his starched white cuffs,
hide my shame in a drawer,
but on good days

ah, the good days! when
justice is not only done
but appears to be done

I feel proud, snuggle up
in his breast pocket, secure
in the knowledge

I'm a somebody, that my life
has meaning after all.

Believe Me Judge, There Are Days When I Can Hardly Believe Myself

The owner of the motorcycle,
one of those people who
keeps scrupulous records,
testified that the odometer
on the bike at the time of the
theft was 25,821 kilometres.

When police searched the
accused's basement, they found,
among several parts belonging
to the same model and year as
the stolen bike, an odometer
with the same reading.

"I bought the odometer for
$150 at a swap sale several
months ago, I wanted
to upgrade my old bike." Though

he didn't get a receipt
and couldn't remember the
vendor, he noted the odometer
reading: 58,321 kilometres.
"I decided to roll it back to
zero just for fun."

He explained how he used a
reversible hand drill and logged
39 hours—he used up 35 batteries—
to roll back the numbers until he
lost interest.

"But isn't it a remarkable coincidence
that you gave up precisely at the
odometer reading of the stolen bike?"

"Believe me judge," the accused said,
with big, guileless eyes,
"there are days when I can hardly
believe myself."

True Calling

There's fire in the courts!
Lawyers are combusting,
water jugs evaporating,
precious precedents are going up
                                        in smoke.

I barricade myself
                                        in chambers,
surrounded by my zebra plants
and African violets,
sword ferns, dieffenbachia,
Japanese jade
                                        and English ivy,
refuse to leave.

I think I've found
                                        my true calling—
watering the green poetry of words,
growing wings.

Jailhouse Blues

Sky diver
dove of my desire
remember I am here & not else-
where in this harlequin disguise,
stone-faced maze.

Broken-winged fly impaled
on this dunghill,
I squirm
in steel shavings & puke, watching
Christ spin on the cross.

O holier than thou-ness
in your merry-go-
roundness
do you hear what I say? or
does your mind turn away?

Blue velvet darkness cleaves
like a magnet;
alone & lonely—my books of escape
all read, I close
my eyes & dream, weave
through the night like a wolf.
You white-collar stiffs
in your rocking-horse coffins
don't you hear me
circling your nests?

Sky diver
dove of desire, please tell me:
how long's the night's journey?
will I ever find rest? &
                                        if I could convince you
death was the answer
                                        would you?
If you know what I mean.

Judges

Not birds of paradise
coo-cooing in their golden crests,

or randy crows
cawing on hot pavements,

but emperor penguins,
who never waddle

from their rookeries.
Even the white plumes

of humpbacks on the horizon
can't nudge them

from their closed circles.

Coffee Break

After he let Winkie the black Lab out, the judge
sat down at the breakfast table & opened the
morning paper. CRIME IN FREEFALL
This was no canard. For months headlines had
cast a long shadow over his colleagues on the bench.
He phoned the police. "What's going on Chief?" but
the chief nonplussed, suggested a spiritual revolution
was afoot. With courtrooms deserted he & his colleagues
polished old judgments, redecorated their chambers etc.
concealing their foreboding under a façade of quips
about "going on the dole." Everyone knew a crisis
loomed: a torrent of letters & e-mail harping on judges'
salaries, accusing them of idleness. They began
to consume quantities of coffee, experimenting with exotic
beans & roasts. After a few weeks their usually erudite
discourse was reduced to squabbles over Colombian
Excelso versus Kenyan AA, Full City versus Italian roast etc.
sounding more & more like jumpy addicts, wide awake, yet
unbelievably tired.

Verdict

As he left the housewarming he made
a quick calculation; three, maybe

four beers, two toasts of champagne,
the "one for the road"—a scotch

on the rocks. Too close for comfort,
he thought, remembering the legion

of hapless drivers he'd sentenced for
crossing the line. But he decided

to take a chance. Halfway down
Waterloo Ave. he realized too late that

the commotion on the road was not
an accident, but the RIDE PROGRAM and

the police were out in force, domelights
whirling, stopping everyone. His stomach

clenched, hands trembled. An officer
waved a red flashlight, he pulled to

the side of the road. "Just a couple,"
he heard himself saying, scarcely believing

he'd just uttered the courtroom cliché
he'd heard a thousand times

—a sure indicia of guilt.
For a second he thought of saying he was

a judge but immediately rejected the
idea. Some officers, he knew, would

have no mercy on a judge who broke the
law and besides he'd always believed

in equality. The officer produced
the ROADSIDE SCREENING DEVICE,

inserted a fresh plastic mouthpiece:
he knew he had no choice.

Heart pounding, he took a deep
breath and blew, then closed his eyes,

waited for the verdict.

Most of the Time

you don't need a crystal ball
to know exactly where you
intend to go even before the
case is over.
But after a close custody battle
or when you have to sentence
a first offender,
you leave the courtroom,
your mind a blizzard,
wondering how you'll ever
find a way
through that whiteness.

Black and White

My old aunt hated drugs,
believed they would be the ruination
of youth, and wanted every drug
trafficker nailed to the cross.

At least that's the way she felt before
I took her to court that Monday morning
for the sentencing of an eighteen-year-
old who had pleaded guilty to selling hash
in the washroom of the high school.
"I'd lock him up and throw away
the key," she said.

But later when she saw the broken
faces of the mother and father
(he was an only son) and heard the boy
testify in a choking voice how he got
hooked (a pusher at the local pool hall had
introduced him to pot when he was fourteen),
that he had to sell to feed his coke
habit, and that he hated himself for all the
pain he had caused his mom and dad, she
changed her mind.

At the morning break, she came to my
chambers unannounced, jaw set,
and pleaded with me to give the boy a break.
"Remember, he's a victim too," she said, as
I ushered her out of the office.

The End of Something

Why did the waiting always seem so long?
All day she had tiptoed around
the apartment as though he was already

there, sleeping somewhere, and the
least noise would waken him. She made
herself tea for the fourth time,
sat on the edge of the beige couch in the
living room, knees clapped together. She could

hear the faucet dripping in the kitchen,
a fly buzzing at the window pane. She
went over, drew back the curtain.
He parked the blue Pontiac in
front of the apartment and let it idle
a few minutes before he got out.

She remembered
the first time he had ordered her to take
off her sweater and bra. "Nice tits," he said,
staring at her small, white body.
All she could recall
was his shallow, rapid breathing,
the rancid smell of his oily skin

and the bluntness of his knee
wedging apart her legs. When he was
finished he strolled around the apartment as
though nothing had happened. "It's a pigsty
in here Jeannie," he said.

She could never look him
in the eye and her only
recollection of their brief encounters was
the skull and crossbones on his silver

buckle, the black cowboy boots, and
riff of his zipper. She felt like
carrion, the same deadweight feeling she had
back home in Nova Scotia when he used to
sneak upstairs to her bedroom

after Mom and Dad were asleep and she would
stare at the dark ceiling, heart pounding,
waiting for his rough hands to reach
under the cover to touch her body.

Today she knelt on the Chinese rug
on the living room floor, arms
criss-crossed over her chest,
waiting for the knock.

That evening when her boyfriend found her
she was still there,
speared by slanting light,
moaning like a golden doe.

White Feather

During morning break
his deputy came to him
in Chambers
holding a long
white feather.
"I found it in the
courtroom," she said,
astonished
as though evidence
of a bird on the wing
had no place
in the halls of
Justice.
"I wonder where it came from."

Sentencing

I wonder
if people like Billy—the big,
swarthy man with burning eyes
who appears before me
PROUD TO BE MOHAWK stamped on his sweat-
shirt—will ever cease to be a displaced
person;

I remember when
men like Billy stole into town Saturday
mornings to peddle
pickerel and mudcat
door to door
for dimes,
their breath reeking of rye and
children mocked them with war cries
just like in the cowboy movies.

It's true
that Billy's parents were alcoholics,
that his dad abandoned them when he was
five,
that he can barely read or write,
that he drinks too much for his own good,
that he carries a log on his
shoulder,

but all the sensitivity training in the world
won't help Billy today,
who crossed the centre line and smashed
another car, putting the driver in
hospital with a broken leg,
now convicted for the fourth time
of impaired driving;
"I have no choice, but to send
you to jail for a long time," I say.

But deterrence is only white
man's bullshit to Billy,
so I quickly do what I have to do
and leave,
wondering if Billy thinks he's being screwed again
by white man's justice.

In the hallway my constable smirks:
"That was one surprised Indian."
I glare at his pale, smug face,
until I see myself
reflected back.

The Gate

(for R.G. Thomas)

After he delivered a judgment (and before
his next case) the judge
liked to retreat to his chambers, cover
his eyes
        with a black silk mask &
take a nap.

He'd see a gate
        open, golden, wide,
a guardian angel graven on its side,
a scene so bright,
        it filled his dream with light,
but when he woke the gate
        was always gone

as though his sleeve had smudged the slate
        leaving him,
brightness dimmed,
frailties intact
        to walk alone
the long dark hall.

Minnows

All eyewitnesses agreed
that the day of the accident
was warm and sunny.

The victim testified that
she entered the intersection
on a green light and the accused
struck the front of her car.

The accused testified that
he entered the intersection
on a green light and the victim
struck the front of his car.

The old lady rocking
on the veranda testified
that the accused definitely
ran the red light.

The young man on the Suzuki motorcycle
testified that the accused
definitely stopped
at the red light.

The pensioner strolling on the sidewalk
testified that everything happened so fast
he couldn't say what colour the light was.

The judge remembered another sunny day
at Jackson's Creek and minnows
shimmering past

his small, awkward hands.

A Question Too Far

After the lawyer asked the bespectacled
witness in the blue suit
what he did for a living, silence fell
over the courtroom. The lawyer repeated
the question.
"I'd rather not say," the witness answered.

That's when I stepped in to remind him
that this was a court of law, that witnesses
are obliged to answer all questions.
"To tell the truth, Your Honour," he said
looking me in the eye, "I'm
just putting the finishing touches on my
invention to liquidate the national debt
in two years."
"The national debt in two years?" I said.
"How do you expect to do that?"

The witness smiled at me
as though I were a child. "Now
Your Honour, I wouldn't be much of a
businessman if I tipped my hand, would I?"
"I guess not," I replied. "Mum's the word."

Motion for Possession

He hadn't worked for two and a half years,
he said, his lungs had been poisoned at
work and he'd been on Workman's Compensation
but now their doctors had cut him off,
claimed he was fit to go back to work,
that it was all in his head,
but he knew the gas
was still there and that if he went back
he'd die, which was what
the government and
the Canadian Manufacturers' Association
wanted anyway because he'd spoken out
about this killer gas in the workplace
and now he'd fallen
behind in his mortgage installments
and the Trust Company wanted to put him and
his wife and two girls out on the street and if they take
our home,
my wife said she'd gas herself,
and she means it, believe me, he said,
her life is in your hands, Your Honour.

Pharmacy

In the general pharmacy
                    of the law
shelves brim
with a bright array of
          bromides,
                    balms
                              and assorted
perfumeries
(all exotically labelled and
government endorsed)
to stop your ailments
                    from getting worse.

Revenge (the aroma that never fails),
Divorce, Alimony and Bail,

Partition, Contrition
and Certiori,

Committals, Acquittals
and Palimony,

Annulments, Garnishments
and Equity (in season)

etcetera.

But buyer beware—
there are no money-back guarantees
                                    and the remedies
can kill.

Scapegoat

The killer was behind bars,
the crowd circled
the clapboard bungalow at dawn.

Two grey-toothed backhoes,
snagged wires, mattresses, floor-
boards and plumbing fixtures,
the crowd clapping, eyes exulted,
drywall dust, an incense, rising.

By midday, an eerie silence
as a cortege of trucks
carted away the splintered bones,
the evil spirit sealed under
three feet of topsoil.

The crowd lunged
onto the killing ground,
trampling its own shadow,
delivered to the safety
of its dark innocent world.

Sometimes I Feel Pity

for the not-so-good thief,
you know, the one who leaves finely sculpted
footprints in snowdrifts and perfect fingerprints
on fridge doors, florid calling cards;
the hapless creature
who, nabbed red-handed with the smoldering goods
in the back of the open pickup,
is struck speechless until
at the station
he opens his heart to the first officer
who promises to be his friend,
sealing the alliance
with a signed inculpatory statement;
yes, there has to be a place
in paradise even for the clumsy thief,
whose simplicity
makes us want to forgive,
like Jesus,
his artless mischief.

There Are Days

when being the vowed
upholder of the Law isn't easy.
For instance today
when I dismissed the Bank's
claim—for $13,000
plus accumulated interest—
against a woman
with three small
sons and an alcoholic husband who
hadn't paid support in years
because he couldn't hold a job;
the Bank's case was strong
and the woman, surprised,
broke into tears,
grateful, I suppose,
that someone had finally understood
what it was like out there
alone
in a dingy apartment in the
city, with no savings,
trying to raise three boys
on $25,000 a year and
why she didn't deserve this debt
(even though she'd co-signed the promissory note),
for money her
husband squandered on booze.
No, it isn't easy,

especially when counsel for the Bank
leaps to his feet,
an incredulous look in his eyes,
to demand legal reasons
(which, of course, an Appeal Court
would be entitled to know),
and I have to rack my brain
until I finally say to myself
—the Law's an ass.

Nightscope

Often he'd dream of a pair of perfect
specs spun from translucent gold that
he would hold aloft & wag at wayward
lawyers who dared to wax to bold, lens
so clear & strong that even on the darkest
night, vision rinsed in diamond light—he could
always tell the wrong from right— but

in the morning when he'd wake, the specs
were never there, slipped through the tattered
net of dreams somewhere—a drawer or pocket
who can say—& he would have to crawl on
hands & knees, cope with a world no longer
black & white, fuzzier than an x-ray—
the watery eye of justice, grey.

Report from the Judicial System to the Public

He was an only child and did all the normal things
for a boy his age. Cubs. Scouts. Church League

Hockey. Neighbours remarked on his easy smile and
winsome ways. He loved rock concerts and music videos,

wore baggy pants and expensive sneakers. In high
school he moved with the right crowd

and was popular with the girls. At 14 he started to
smoke grass and drink. He screwed up at school.

He never forgave his father for once hitting him
when he came home drunk. He resented his mother

for always being on his case. Three days before
Christmas and two days after his 17th birthday

he came home one evening with a loaded semi-
automatic .22 and pumped four bullets into each

of their skulls. Afterwards, he treated himself
to a steak dinner downtown with his mom's pin money

before reporting the killings to the police. He
is called a Young Offender, still a teenager with

big, awkward hands and embarrassing zits.
The shrinks will try to figure out what went wrong.

In three years he will be delivered back to you.

Last Outing

At dawn they went fishing, took turns
rowing the old cedar strip skiff; sunlight
dripped from the oars, the oarlocks creaked &
a gull *screed* above the spot where
they anchored. Divvying the fat dew worms
they fished all morning, water striders
creasing the silky water.

Back home they counted out the catch,
half & half. "No strife," they'd always say.
In the afternoon they drove to court,
she in the Ford, he in the Pontiac.
Clean as a boning knife they
carved up the house &
then the children.

Strange Encounters of a New Kind

In the old days
marriages broke up
in the rut of passion,
                                        but the times
they are a-changin':
the distraught husband
seeking interim custody
of three children
because
the wife
planned to leave him
for a woman in Hong Kong,
someone she'd met
surfing
in cyberspace.

A Strange Feeling

As I slash
through stacks of divorce

files on my desk, lopping off
decades of life together,

children, homes, holidays,
good times, foul times,

with a flick of my pen,
I'm trespassing

on holy ground,
and when I see

lilies, turtle doves,
and golden rings on the

scrolled Certificates of Marriage,
the wedding day

comes shining back,
and sad eyes watch

as I scrawl my name
across their ghostly witness.

Saturday's Children

Why don't you join me at Burger King
early Saturday morning for breakfast?

The decor's cheery: a white fluorescent
heaven overhead, the air awash with

no-name music designed to keep
the soul from sinking,

and room dividers of plastic fronds
to conjure up the illusion of

sunnier climes. See, Santa's still
in the window—though Christmas is

now three weeks old—wearing a black
top hat as he leads a line of merry

youngsters up a hill and if you look
carefully you'll see scattered

around the tables some of your
neighbours, regular customers, like me,

who come for the atmosphere and always
eat alone … the haggard woman

across the aisle, stubbing her
fifth cigarette this morning, squinting

at the snow as
though she half expected someone from

her past to emerge from that
swirling silver and, of course, you

mustn't miss the Burger King basement
playground—if you're taller than the

Burger Chipmunk you can't go down—
and Saturday's children, jostling

each other in the plastic ball pit,
frantic, upturned eyes yearning

for attention from weekend fathers,
awkward, behind glass walls.

Fly

During the morning recess
the judge gazed from
his chambers
to the bleak November sky
above the Niagara mountain.

The two men had picked her up
on Jarvis Street,
drove to a field north
of the city;
afterward, the crown said,
they slit her throat.

Observing a fly
on the windowpane trapped inside
the judge grabbed a newspaper
cocked his arm,
                                        then froze,
shocked at the violence
within him.

Vigilante Justice

She lived with a group of six women,
she said, all student nurses like herself.
One told them how she had been sexually
assaulted in the parking lot of the nursing
residence. Somehow they suspected the
perpetrator would return to the scene &
when he showed up a week later, they
were ready.

"Before he knew what was happening
we'd surrounded his car," she said.
"I still remember his small, dark
moustache, the way his upper lip
trembled. He tried to run but we had
baseball bats & crowbars & swarmed him.
Sometimes at night I shudder at
how we left him on the pavement, naked
& unconscious, but still alive."

She paused, took a sip of wine.
"I can't tell you what happened to him
after that," she said. "I only know he'll
never rape again."

Caught in the Net

Only three days into this trial
and already I'm in a sweat,

for it's apparent that the
Plaintiff, small fish in a big sea,

will be swallowed bones and all
by Leviathan Trust Company

whom he dared to bite. As judge
I cling to the raft

of impartiality, hoping for a miracle,
—that the Plaintiff, like Jonah, will

escape unscathed but, alas, it is not to be.
My plea to settle is rejected and God,

it appears, is in no mood for miracles.
The case rolls on like a tidal wave

as the net closes and I resign myself
to my role—

eviscerating shark of justice.

The Cardinal Judicial Sin

Most believe that judging
is a glamorous profession,
but the truth is more earthy,
like the near drowning
I experienced in a flood case,
listening to lawyers and
experts gurgle on about flood
plains, geodetic elevations,
hydraulics, meteorological data,
Manning equations, mudslides,
culverts, ditches, inverts,
field tile, contour lines,
benchmarks, gradients, snowmelts,
(etc.),
until my backside began to freeze
and I felt like sentencing
every windbag in the courtroom
for the crime of boredom.

But judges are constrained
to listen to every nerve-numbing syllable
and to fall asleep
is the cardinal judicial sin
as the unlucky judge on the East coast
discovered recently
when he was reprimanded

by the Judicial Council
for dozing off
at the end of a hard day,
when all the poor devil wanted to do,
like me,
was save his sanity.

The Last Straw

Judge Highcastle hated criminals. His idea
of a good day in court was to send as many
as he could to the slammer. Priscilla, his wife,
advised him to lighten up, but over the years he
saw a world strewn with criminal intentions,
spent hours in front of the blue box
in the basement watching *American Justice* &
America's Most Wanted & other programs
on law & order, seldom getting to sleep before 3 am.

Priscilla was caught snitching a Douglas Cuddle Bear,
from Toys R Us at the local mall. Something snapped.
The judge sits by his pond, cuts off the
legs of bullfrogs, their quiet, bulging eyes
asking why? Occasionally, the neighbours say, he laughs
the crazy insane laughter of loons.

This Morning

as I drive to the courthouse after a restless night
dreaming about
the man at Pearson airport with the funny shoes
I have two consolations:
my Isoflex exercise ball and the Butler GUM
stimulator with brass handle and
orange tip Thérèse gave me, you don't want to be
an old man with dentures do you? she said long ago
I stopped listening
to the radio news only makes me blue and cranky,
I spy a porcupine
sliced in two on the Hanlon, the sun burning through
a creamy bank of sky
I'm travelling the limit but drivers with power suits
and cigars are whizzing by talking
to their phones if I ever become a millionaire
I'll buy myself
a gold cellular and plug into the universe in style—
GOODBYE ISOLATION!

In the lunchroom I pour myself a buttermilk wait
for Nick to appear
with the latest jokes from the Internet my friends used
to say I had a happy-go-lucky demeanour,
in the courtroom photos the shoes looked normal,
the immigration office testified, but when they
peeled away the soles
they found sealed compartments with hash

a professional job, said the crown,
have mercy, the wife cried, he's just a poor guy
with four kids &
then Nick sails in to announce he's put the last
of the jury charges on his desktop,
takes one look at me and stops, we judges should
never second guess ourselves,
no wonder we've got ulcers etc. etc. and we both agree
that Clinton's shenanigans
are giving the Presidency a bad rap
that the glut of sexual assault cases
is making us miserable that 15 years on the bench
is penance enough & Nick says he'd like
to spend his retirement fixing up
big-finned Detroit cars and I tell him I want to write
a family memoir if
the Feds ever come through with our promised raise and I say
to him, I got an anonymous letter
signed by *John Q. Public*
informing me that beyond question
I was the worst judge in Canada &
that if I had even a sliver of self-respect
I'd resign.

How to Bribe a Judge

Snap to attention when he enters the
courtroom and never fail to say:
"GOOD MORNING."

Smile—make him feel welcome as a lover.

Laugh heartily at all his jokes even when
they're incomprehensible.

When he says something particularly absurd
chime in: "I wish I'd thought of that."

Ponder deeply—learn the art of furrowing the
brow or staring gravely at the ceiling—
especially when he's talking silly.

Without appearing obsequious finish every
sentence with "My Lord."

Quote with boldness from his old decisions
no matter how dull, irrelevant or wrong.

When he's patently confused, interject:
"Would you mind repeating that My Lord,
I missed the subtlety of it." Or try a
variation: "You're one step ahead of me
as usual My Lord."

Tell him his judgments are novel, break
new ground. Avoid meretricious adjectives
like "brilliant"; he'll know it's flattery.

Send him a Christmas card, expressing
gratitude for his birth.

Never offer cash—his dignity will be
slighted.

Finally, never appeal his judgments.

Night Moth

Between stars and screen
the moth
with iridescent body
and seven white notches
on delta wings,
                    listens
to the cantillations
of the frogs,
prisoner like me,
caught in the shadows.

Judge's Lament

There is a field
beyond
ideas
of rightdoing
and wrongdoing
where the soul
can lie down among
wildflowers
and lack nothing,
but
I can't meet you there;
and the field
is far away
in another country.

(after Rumi)

My thanks to Barry Callaghan
for selecting and editing this collection,
to Margaret Oldfield
again for her diligent assistance
and to Susan Musgrave
for showing me that poetry was a possibility.

Other Books

by

James Clarke

The Ancient Pedigrees of Plums

Silver Mercies

The Raggedy Parade

The Way Everyone Is Inside